D1383331

TRUSSVILLE PUBLIC LIBRARY
201 PARKWAY DRIVE
TRUSSVILLE, ALA. 35173
(205) 655-2022

WITHDRAWN

Touch

See for Yourself

Touch

Brenda Walpole
Photographs by Barrie Watts

RSVP
RAINTREE
STECK-VAUGHN
P U B L I S H E R S
The Steck-Vaughn Company

Austin, Texas

TRUSSVILLE PUBLIC LIBRARY

© Copyright 1997, text, Steck-Vaughn Company

All rights reserved. No part of this book may be reproduced or utilized in any form or by any means, electronic or mechanical, including photocopying, recording, or by any information storage and retrieval system, without permission in writing from the Publisher. Inquiries should be addressed to: Copyright Permissions, Steck-Vaughn Company, P.O. Box 26015, Austin, TX 78755

Published by Raintree Steck-Vaughn Publishers, an imprint of Steck-Vaughn Company

Editor: Kathy DeVico
Project Manager: Amy Atkinson
Electronic Production: Scott Melcer

All photographs by Barrie Watts except for:
p. 9 Sally Lancaster/RNIB; p. 11 Lois Joy Thurston/Bubbles Photolibrary; p. 13 Tony Freeman/PhotoEdit; p. 21 John Heinrich/Zul Colour Library; p. 25 Jane Knights/Zul Colour Library

Library of Congress Cataloging-in-Publication Data
Walpole, Brenda.
    Touch / Brenda Walpole; photographs by Barrie Watts.
        p.   cm. — (See for yourself)
    Includes index.
    Summary: Introduces the concept of touch and suggests activities which reinforce the understanding of this sense.
    ISBN 0-8172-4216-3
    1. Touch — Juvenile literature.   [1. Touch.   2. Senses and sensation.]   I. Watts, Barrie, ill.   II. Title.   III. Series.
QP451.W25   1997
612.8'8 — dc20   96-6173
                                                                         CIP
                                                                         AC

Printed and bound in the United States
1 2 3 4 5 6 7 8 9 0 LB 99 98 97 96

Contents

Exploring with Touch

One way to find out about things is to feel them with your hands.

The girl in the big picture is using her sense of touch to learn about the model. She can feel its shape and size. She can feel where the model is rough, smooth, or bumpy.

You could try testing a friend's sense of touch. Find some empty boxes. Cut a hole in each lid. Choose a different object to put into each box. You could try sandpaper, soap, and some cloth. Ask a friend to feel inside the box without looking. Can he or she guess what is inside? Can he or she describe how it feels?

Fingertips

Our fingertips are so sensitive that we can feel a single human hair. Fingertips can feel the difference between curly hair and straight hair, or thick hair and fine hair.

Many blind people use their fingertips to read. They learn to use a special alphabet, called braille. Each letter of this alphabet is made up of a pattern of tiny bumps on the page. Braille readers can feel the bumps with their fingers.

Can you read with your fingertips? Write some numbers on a piece of paper using a glue stick. Sprinkle fine sand over the glue. When it is dry, shake off any loose sand. Close your eyes, and take turns with a friend trying to read the numbers by using your fingers.

What Are Nerves?

A network of long, thin threads runs all through your body. These threads are called nerves. Nerves carry messages to and from your brain. The nerves that end in your skin give you a sense of touch.

When you touch something, the nerves respond by sending a message to your brain. Your brain then sorts out the message and figures out what you are touching. Some nerves sense heat and cold. Other nerves sense roughness or smoothness, pain or pressure.

Your hands, lips, and tongue all have lots of nerves. Babies learn about new things by feeling them and putting them into their mouths.

Try this test to find out which areas of your body have the most nerve endings. Tape two pencils together. Close your eyes. Ask a friend to gently touch different areas of your body with the two pencil points. You will feel both pencil points where you have the most nerves. Where there are fewer nerves, you'll only feel one point.

Hot and Cold

How do you test the water in a swimming pool, before you get in it? It's important to know if it will be too cold for you. Testing the water with your hand or toe will tell you if the water is the right temperature for a swim.

It can be dangerous for the body to become too hot or too cold. This is why you have nerves in your skin that detect heat and cold.

When the weather is very cold, you shiver and get goose bumps. You may decide to wear extra clothes to warm up. In the summer, you wear fewer clothes. If it is very hot, you might sweat. This cools you down.

The nerves in your skin check your body temperature constantly. Your body stays at the right temperature, about 98.6°F (37°C), whatever the weather, and whatever you are doing.

Pain and Pressure

Pain is important. It warns you that something is wrong and that you must do something to stop the pain. Pinching or squeezing your skin hurts. This is because it affects the nerves that sense pain. The pressure of a tight shoe or of a pin sticking into you can be very painful.

But not all pressure is painful. You feel a gentle pressure when clothes are resting against your body, or if you hold a ball in your hands.

Sometimes in the winter, our fingers get so cold that they get numb. When this happens, we lose our sense of touch. What might happen to you if you could not feel pain or sense hot temperatures?

Try pinching yourself gently on different parts of your body. Are some areas more sensitive to pinching than others?

How Do Animals Feel?

Some animals have long whiskers or tentacles that are extra sensitive to touch. Cats use their whiskers to judge whether gaps are wide enough for them to get through. A cat's whiskers stretch out as wide as its shoulders. When a whisker brushes against a fence or a tree, nerves at the root of the whisker are triggered.

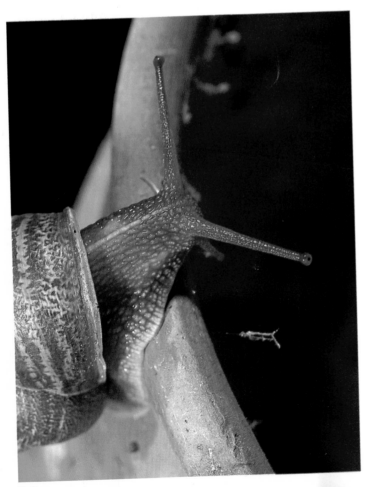

An octopus uses its long tentacles to feel its way around. It feels around corners and into cracks to look for hiding places.

A snail has feelers on its head. Snails use their feelers to find their way around. Watch a snail as it moves along. See how it uses its feelers to touch leaves and stones as it moves forward. What makes the snail pull its feelers in?

How Animals Use Touch

A sea anemone cannot chase its food, because its body is attached to a rock. Its tentacles reach out into the water and feel for any passing animals. First, it stings tiny creatures with its tentacles. Then, the tentacles sweep the creatures into the anemone's mouth.

Many animals feel their food before they choose whether or not to eat it. Monkeys squeeze fruits to see if they are ripe enough to eat. Some fruits, such as peaches, feel soft when they are ripe and sweet. If they feel hard, they will probably not be ripe and will taste sour.

Make a chart of fruits that you might squeeze to see if they are ready to eat. Which ones are best when they are soft? Which ones would you avoid if they were soft?

18

A Delicate Touch

When chefs make pastry dough, they mix the ingredients until the texture feels right. Then they press and shape the dough with their hands until it is soft enough to be rolled out.

The potter in the big picture is using his hands, too. As he touches the clay, he checks that it is not too wet or too dry to shape and model.

Can you think of other people who work with their hands?

Use your hands to make an animal out of modeling clay. Make ears, eyes, and a tail with your fingertips. Could you make the same model if you were wearing gloves? Why would it be much harder to do?

How Our Senses Work Together

Can you thread a needle? While one hand holds the needle steady, the other moves the thread through the loop at the top of the needle. Hands and eyes need to work together on a delicate job like this one.

If you play a musical instrument, such as the violin, your hands work with your senses of sight and hearing. The fingers of one hand press on the strings, while the other hand moves the bow. As you play, your eyes read the music, and your ears listen to what you are playing.

We don't need two hands for all tasks. We write or draw using only one hand. Our sense of touch helps us to hold a pen or pencil firmly. Our eyesight helps to guide our hand across the page.

Showing Our Feelings

It is always safer to hold hands with a grown-up when you cross a road. Holding someone's hand shows that you trust him or her. You may hold hands with your best friends or put your arm around their shoulders. It shows that you like them very much. But if you don't like someone touching you, you can say so.

Grown-ups shake hands with their friends and with people they meet. Families and friends often hug and kiss. Parents cuddle with their children to show that they love them.

Some animals like to be touched, too. Pet dogs and cats like to be stroked or petted. Young animals often snuggle together for warmth and safety.

Fooling Your Senses

Most of the time, your sense of touch is very accurate. However, sometimes your brain receives messages that it cannot understand.

Take three small bowls. Ask an adult to help you fill the first bowl with hot water. Make sure that the water is not too hot. Fill the second bowl with cold water, and the third bowl with warm water.

Dip the fingers of your left hand into the hot water.
Dip the fingers of your right hand into the cold water.

After about 20 seconds, put both hands into the warm water. How does the water feel to each hand?

More Things to Do

1. Touch words
Close your eyes, and touch your own face.
Which touch words can you think of to
describe what you feel?

2. Test your body's sensitivity.
Using a felt-tip pen, mark a grid of 20 dots on
the back of your hand. Ask a friend to gently
touch each dot in turn with a pencil point.
Keep your eyes closed. How many can you
feel? Try the same exercise on your leg or arm.
Which part of the body is most sensitive? Give
the same test to your friend. Who is more
sensitive to this test?

3. Guess the temperature.
Try guessing the temperatures of some things in
your home or classroom, such as a radiator, a
glass of juice, the refrigerator, and hot and cold
water from the faucet. Make a list of your
guesses. Start with the object that you think is
the hottest, and end with the object that you
think is the coolest. Now measure the actual
temperatures with a thermometer. How close
were your guesses?

Index

This index will help you find some
of the important words in this book.

© 1996 A&C Black

Notes for Parents and Teachers

These notes will give you some additional information about the senses and suggest some more activities you might like to try with the children.

Pages 6–9
The nervous system consists of a network of nerves that extends to all parts of the body. A nerve is a bundle of individual nerve fibers. Some nerves carry messages to the brain and spinal cord, which together are the body's coordinating centers. Messages are sent as tiny pulses of electricity. In most cases, these electrical pulses travel up the spinal cord to the brain. Other nerves then carry messages from the brain to the muscles or organs. These will then cause a response.

Pages 10–11
The highest concentration of sensory receptors is in the fingertips, hands, lips, soles of the feet, and genitals. There are several different types of receptors, which respond to pain, pressure, heat and cold, and light touches. Pain receptors are the most common type. The different nerves are found at different depths below the skin.

Pages 12–13
Overstimulation of the pressure and temperature receptors can also result in feelings of pain. Because pain may be a sign of potential damage to the body, the information from pain receptors is processed immediately, often resulting in reflex actions. Reflex actions are instant responses instigated by the spinal cord, not the brain.

We blink automatically if something is approaching and is likely to touch our eyes. However, after repeated false alarms, such as hands being waved in front of the eye, we can control the reflex. The children could form pairs and take turns moving their hands quickly in front of their partner's eyes. How long does it take the children to control the reflex blinking action?

Pages 16–17
Hairs covering the human body also have sensory receptors at the roots. When the hairs are brushed or moved, even by a gentle breeze, they stimulate these receptors.

Snails, which have limited vision, use their feelers to find their way around. Snails retract their feelers on contact with hard objects or certain chemicals, such as salt, which could be harmful to them.

Pages 18–19
Children could investigate how long the ripening process takes in various fruits and find out how suppliers try to slow down or speed up this process so that the food we buy is ready to eat.

Pages 26–27
In the experiment, nerves in both hands sense that the temperature of the water has changed. However, the different messages from each hand confuse the brain.

4.2/.5

TRUSSVILLE PUBLIC LIBRARY
201 PARKWAY DRIVE
TRUSSVILLE, AL 35173-1125
(205) 655-2022

GAYLORD